Exiled in the West
The Mystical Narration of Shihab al-Din Suhrawardi's *Recital of the Occidental Exile*

Translated by

Laleh Bakhtiar
and
Gholamreza Aavani

Great Books of the Islamic World

Printed in the United States of America.
Library of Congress Cataloguing-in-Publication Data
Laleh Bakhtiar, Gholamreza Aavani

Exiled in the West: The Mystical Narration of
Shihab al-Din Suhrawardi's "Recital of the Occidental Exile"
1. Islam. 2. Sufism. I. Title II. Author

ISBN 10: 1-56744-671-X
ISBN 13: 978-1-56744-671-5

Cover design: Liaquat Ali
  Cornerstones are Allah and Muhammad connected by *Bismillah al-Rahman al-Rahim* (In the Name of God, the Merciful, the Compassionate).
  Logo design by Mani Ardalan Farhadi. The cypress tree bending with the wind, the source for the paisley design, is a symbol of the perfect Muslim, who, as the tree, bends with the wind of God's Will.

Published by
Great Books of the Islamic World

Distributed by
Kazi Publications, Inc
3023 West Belmont Avenue
Chicago IL 60618
(T) 773-267-7001; (F) 773-267-7002
email: info@kazi.org www.kazi.org

Contents

In the Name of God, the Merciful, the Compassionate

Preface

My journey through Shihab al-Din Suhrawardi's mystical recitals began in 1970 in Tehran, Iran. While I was born in Tehran, when I was six months old, my American mother brought me to America. Growing up with a single-parent American mother, I never learned Persian. I returned to Iran when I was twenty-four with an Iranian husband, Nader Ardalan, and two daughters. While I was taking classes in English at Tehran University on Sufism and Islamic culture taught by Seyyed Hossein Nasr, my main mission had been to learn Persian. Dr. Nasr introduced Professor Gholamreza Aavani to me to teach me Persian.

Being a philosopher, Dr. Aavani thought "outside the box" and snuggested I could learn Persian by reading and translating the 12th century mystical recitals of Suhrawardi as the Persian language had not changed over the centuries.

This opened doors to me not only to learn to read Persian, but to Islamic mysticism as well. Known in the West as Sufism, there is also a dimension known as Irfan (gnosis) whereby the mystic to be develops his or her intuitions and gathered experiential knowledge. As a result, as I wrote in my journals of those years: I am having illuminative dreams. I asked Seyyed Hossein Nasr, at that time a professor of philosophy as well as a practicing Sufi/Arif, what my having spiritual dreams meant. He said to me in 1974 that I was on the verge of spiritual reintegration and that I was learning Irfan from him.[1] I spoke to my brother, Jamshid, a practicing Jungian psychiatrist and he said, as I recorded in my journal, that I was going through individuation.

Dr. Aavani and I translated all nine of the mystical recitals as well as the anonymous Persian commentary on "The Recital of the Occidental Exile." Here, only the "Recital of the Occidental Exile" is published. The rest are, God willing, awaiting traditional commentaries.

When Professor Henry Corbin published the original Arabic of "The Recital of the Occidental Exile" he also included the only commentary found to date on this Recital, an anonymous, early Persian commentary. Professor Corbin has also commented extensively upon these recitals, in particular, "The Recital of the Occidental Exile." This is available to those who read French.

There is also an English translation in a collected by W. M. Thackston, published in 1999 by Mazda Publishers, *The Philosophical Allegories and Mystical Treatises*, along with the Persian translation of this Recital from the original Arabic.

However, neither Corbin nor Thackston reflect on the Quranic references by Suhrawardi. After completing the translations of the mystical recitals of Shihab al-Din Yahya Suhrawardi and due to the fact that he quotes thirty-four Quranic verses in this "Recital of the Occidental Exile" alone, it became apparent that a Quranic commentary was necessary for the English reading audience. The full beauty of the mystical recitals of the Master of Illumination requires a commentary giving the sense of the traditions about which he writes. Just as a stem is the transition between a flower's roots and its flowers, so a mystical treatise cannot grow without a traditional commentary connecting its roots to its potential flowering in the consciousness of the reader.

Recognizing that the link to Suhrawardi's use of Quranic verses needed to be further clarified with a traditional Quranic commentary, many of the verses he uses have often been quoted by Arifs (Muslim Gnostics). Could this link not be strengthened with full explanation of these verses?

But which Quranic commentary to choose? Unfortunately, Suhrawardi himself never wrote a commentary upon the Quran for us to refer to. However, commentaries upon the Quran in Arabic and Persian are innumerable. Putting aside the purely exoteric interpretations, one is still left with an overwhelming number of esoteric commentaries.

Perhaps the difference between an exoteric and esoteric commentary upon the Quran should be further explained here. Stated simply, an exoteric interpretation helps to explain the Shariah, the Divine Law, whereas an esoteric interpretation helps to explain the Way (Tariqah), which leads one to the Truth (Haqiqah). The relationship between the Truth, the Way and the Law may be related through an analogy to a circle. The Law is the circumference, the Way is the radii leading to the center, the center is the Truth, much in the same way with a circle being "self," our body can be seen as the circumference, our soul as the radii leading to the center of the circle, the center being our spirit/intellect.

The central postulate of the mystical Way, the point where one pierces the circumference in order to move towards "centering," is the thesis that there is a hidden meaning in all things. It is through this hidden meaning that all things relate. Here is oneness, unity. Outward forms are illusions, multiplicities covering the inner essence of a thing. One needs to go beyond the form in order to understand essence.

Suhrawardi, as you will read in Professor Corbin's description that follows below, was martyred because of his esoteric position. Therefore, in order to seek further meaning in his words, one needs to look at the radii of the circle, the esoteric interpretation which includes a spiritual hermeneutics for the one who would be guided.

The choice of an esoteric commentary became easier when observing the historical-philosophical tradition between the three great masters, Avicenna (980-1037), Suhrawardi (1154-1191) and Ibn Arabi (1165-1240).[2]

While Avicenna's philosophy plays a major role in Suhrawardi's theosophy, Avicenna was only drawn to the esoteric world in his later years.[3] Suhrawardi stated that there are two legs upon which one must walk: reason and spiritual vision or intuition which has nothing to do with instinct. Intuition results from the light or illumination of consciousness. One must, however, train reason through learning grammar, mathematic, geometry and Peripatetic[4] philosophy according to Suhrawardi at the same time that one is purifying one's consciousness (*tazkiyat al-qalb*).[5] No true philosophy is worthy of one's endeavors unless it combines a spiritual transformation as theosophy is to "become" not to just "think."

Suhrawardi, then, begins where Avicenna left off as he himself states in his preface to "The Recital of the Occidental Exile."

It remains to relate Suhrawardi to the school of Ibn Arabi. We turn to Professor Henry Corbin for the explanation of this relationship.

Suhrawardi, born in Sunni Iran (Iran up to the 16th century was Sunni), was a follower of the Shafi'i law, died a martyr at the age of thirty eight in Aleppo in (1191), a victim of the intolerance of the doctors of the Law and of Salahaddin, known to the Crusaders as Saladin. Though his life was cut off too soon, he succeeded in carrying out a great design in reviving the wisdom of the ancient Persians, their doctrine of Light and Darkness in Sunni Iran. The result was the philosophy, or rather, to take the Arabic term in its etymological sense, the "theosophy of light" (*hikmat al-ishraq*) to which we find parallels in many pages of the work of Ibn Arabi. In accomplishing this great design, Suhrawardi was conscious of establishing "Oriental wisdom" or wisdom of the East to which Avicenna too had aspired and knowledge of which reached Roger Bacon in the thirteenth century. But of this work of Avicenna only fragments remain, and Suhrawardi was of the opinion that because Avicenna was without knowledge of the sources of ancient Iranian wisdom, he had been unable to complete his project.

The effects of Suhrawardi's theosophy of Light have been felt in Iran down to our own time. One of its essential features is that it makes philosophy and mystical experience inseparable. A philosophy that does not culminate in a metaphysic of ecstasy is vain speculation. A mystical experience that is not grounded on a sound philosophical education is in danger of degenerating and going astray.

This element in itself would suffice to place Suhrawardi and Ibn Arabi in the same spiritual family. It situates this theosophy on a spiritual plane higher than the rational plane on which the relations between theology and philosophy, belief and knowledge, are ordinarily discussed. The controversy concerning these relations, so characteristic of postmedieval Western philosophy, has its sources in the situation briefly analyzed above. Actually, Suhrawardi deals not with a problem but with an imperative of the soul—the fusion of philosophy and spirituality.... The disciples of Suhrawardi, *ishraqiyun*, are designated as "Platonists" (*ashab aflatun*). Ibn Arabi was to be surnamed the Platonist, the "son of Plato" (Ibn Aflatun). This clarifies certain co-ordinates of the spiritual topography which we are here trying to establish.

The event which followed the system of Avicenna was not the destruction of his Neoplatonism by the Aristotelian Averroes but the inauguration by Suhrawardi of the theosophy of Light (*hikmat al-ishraq*) as "Oriental wisdom." The determining influence on Sufism and spirituality was not Ghazzali's critique, but the esoteric doctrine of Ibn Arabi and his school.

Furthermore, the spiritual ferment arising from the coalescence of these two schools, that of Suhrawardi's *ishraq* and that of Ibn Arabi's irfan, created a situation which was to lend crucial importance to the relations between Sufism and Shiism. The significance of both these currents in Islam was clarified, the one throwing light on the other....[6]

Therefore, because of the closeness of thought between Suhrawardi and the school of Ibn Arabi, the famous *Tafsir al-Quran al-Karim* by the Shaykh al-Akbar, Muhyi al-Din Ibn Arabi was chosen. Although actually written by 'Abd al Razzaq al-Kashani (b1252-61-d1329-35), a follower of Ibn' Arabi's school, Kashani's commentary is the continuation of the chain of transmission of which he himself was a part. This commentary will be referred to as TQK. It is a commentary which relates verses to their traditional meaning for the inner seeking of self. Solomon or Moses becomes consciousness (*qalb, nafs al-mulhamah*),[7] Noah's Ark, the Divine Law, the hoopoe, inspiration and so on. The steps and stages of the journey are constantly recalled for one who has eyes to see.

*****

Here, the reader first encounters the text in full as written by Suhrawardi. The words in italics are the Quranic verses,[8] the words of which he uses to express his recital. No break in the flow occurs by this means and if they were not in italics, the reader would think the words were Suhrawardi's alone.

The second part contains the translation and commentary. A traditional commentary upon a text often appears as an 'asides' or marginal notes. A master would read, for example, the mystical poem of the 12th century Persian poet, Shabistari, called *Golshan-i-Raz* (Garden of Secrets).[9] Then in the same volume he would find Lahiji's 14th century commentary upon the poem which includes evidence from other poets, prophetic traditions, the Quranic verses, etc. The person reading this would comment in the margin upon the words of Lahiji upon the words of Shabistari. This would remain a great source of knowledge for the disciple.

The commentary upon "The Recital of the Occidental Exile" also varies. If a Quranic verse is referred to by Suhrawardi, the commentary first includes the complete verse of the Quran. Then follows a commentary translated from the Arabic of the TQK. If no Quranic verse is indicated in the text, the commentary is a translation of the anonymous Persian commentary.[10] Following that, certain very pertinent and enlightening passages of Henry Corbin's work *En*

Islam Iranien[11] (EII) are translated from the French and included.

While Suhrawardi wrote this Recital in Arabic, the anonymous commentator wrote his commentary in Persian. The entire Quranic verse to which Suhrawardi refers in two or three words is included along with the translations from the Arabic of the relevant commentary upon that particular verse from the TQK, the notes of the Persian commenttor and the inclusion of some of H. Corbin's comments from English and French.

In the final part, Seyyed Hossein Nasr recapitulates Suhrawardi's story of the Arif exiled in the West.

*****

The "Recital of the Occidental Exile," describes the journey of the "prepared heart," that is, consciousness (*qalb, nafs al-mulhamah*). One could say it is the journey of the false self or ego to the real Self or from the animal soul (*nafs al-ammarah*) to the human soul (*nafs al-insaniyyah*).

We should be very careful to point out at the outset that there is a profound correspondence between the microcosm and the macrocosm in all traditional wisdom. It is due to this that the inward journey of one to the center of one's being corresponds to a journey through the various stages of the universe and finally beyond. For the seeker to escape from the lower soul and move towards the center is also to pass beyond the crypt of the cosmos.

The word "exile" refers to the soul of the seeker which was cast into a physical mold and thereby placed in exile from its origin. As awareness comes to the soul, the sensible-perceptive aspects of the body are pushed aside by a yearning that increases, a yearning to return to whence it had come.

Thus, this is the story of the exiled soul imprisoned in the cosmic crypt of the Occident (the West). The word Occident refers to the material world as opposed to the spiritual. In the cosmology of Suhrawardi, it encompasses the universe from the heaven of the fixed stars (the zodiacal signs) down to the descent of earthly bodies.

This is the place where the latitudinal-longitudinal orders meet and the veils become increasingly denser as they reach to the earth. Suhrawardi further envisions the whole of the universe which is visible to the naked eye as being essentially a cosmic crypt. This world is darkness in comparison to the world beyond the visible. The stars are as windows to the world of lights being but openings to that other world.

This same cosmology is related to the human form. It must undergo certain processes in order to seek the openings and finally the lighted path of escape. It is the soul which is the exile, imprisoned in a physical mold, exiled to the Occident, the material world, returning to its origin in the Orient (the East), the world of light.

Laleh Bakhtiar
Chicago, May, 2019

Endnotes to the Preface

1. *Laleh Bakhtiar, Ph.D. Letters Volume 5.* Published by Kazi Publications, Chicago, 2019.

2 These three men form the basis of Seyyed Hossein Nasr's book, *Three Muslim Sages.* One needs only to refer to it to see the great link.

3. Theosophy refers to philosophy combined with purification of consciousness (*tazkiyat al-qalb*).

4. The development of peripatetic philosophy essentially belongs to Avicenna. It literally means "he who walks" after Aristotle who is said to have given lectures while walking. In the Islamic world, these philosophers, in the Islamic world, considered themselves to be followers of Aristotle, but not in a pure sense. They actually developed Aristotelian philosophy as seen through Neoplatonic eyes in the context of Islamic revelation.

5. See *Quranic Psychology of the Self: A Textbook on Islamic Moral Psychology* by Laleh Bakhtiar. Published by Kazi Publications, 2019.

6. H. Corbin, *Avicenna and the Visionary Recitals*, pp 42-43. See also pages 36-42.

7. See *Quranic Psychology of the Self: A Textbook on Islamic Moral Psychology* by Laleh Bakhtiar. Published by Kazi Publications, 2019.

8. All Quranic verses are translations from *The Sublime Quran*, unless otherwise indicated.

9. This great mystical poem, *Golshan-i raz*, composed in the 13th century, A.D. contains, in summary, form, the doctrines of Sufism. It is written in the *mathnavi* style. Every verse is like a jewel within the total crystalline form.

10. Written anonymously, the Persian translation of "The Recital of the Occidental Exile," as well as the commentary, appears in H. Corbin, *Oeuvres philosophiques et mystiques de Shihabbadin Yahya Sohrawardi.*

11. H. Corbin, *En Islam iranien*, II, *Sohrawardi et les Platoniciens de Perse* and AVR.

Part One: The Translation
"The Recital of the Occidental Exile"
In the Name of God, the Merciful, the Compassionate

Prolog

Thanks be to God who is the Creator of the world and blessings upon the servants whom He chose, especially upon our Sayyid, Muhammad, peace and the mercy of God be upon him, the Chosen one, his family and friends, all.

When I was reading the "Recital of Hayy ibn Yaqzan," in spite of the admirable spiritual thoughts and the profound suggestions which it contained, I found it void of lights which indicate *the Greater Catastrophe*, in other words, the great "stage," which is stored in the Divine Books, concealed in the symbols of the sages and hidden in the "Recital of Salman and Absal," which was composed by the same author who wrote "Hayy ibn Yaqzan." It is this secret on which are based the spiritual stations of the Sufis and of those who possess mystical intuition.

In the "Story of Hayy ibn Yaqzan" as well, there are no indications of this except at the end of the book where it says: Sometimes certain 'unveilers' among men emigrate towards Him, etc. Thus, it was for this reason that I decided to mention a small part of that in a story that I call the "Recital of the Occidental Exile," dedicated to some of my noble friends. For my intention, I trust in God.

The Beginning

I traveled with my brother, 'Asim, from Transoxiana to the countries of the Occident (West) so that we could hunt a group of birds along the shore of the Green Sea. We suddenly fell into *this town whose people are ones who are unjust*, the city of Qayrawan . The inhabitants of the city became aware of our arrival. They realized we were the sons of Shaykh Hadi ibn al-Khayr, the Yemenite. They surrounded us and bound us in chains and shackles of iron and imprisoned us in a well whose depth was fathomless. There was directly above that well, unoccupied until peopled by our presence, a high castle fortified by a number of towers. They told us: You are not forbidden to go up to the castle alone at night, but when day comes, you must fall again into the bottom of the well where there were *shadows some above some others. When we put forth our hands wellnigh we could not see them.*

During the night hours we climbed to the castle, dominating the immensity of space as we looked down through an opening. Frequently doves of the forests of Yemen came and informed us of the state of things in the sacred region. Sometimes we were also visited by lights from Yemen, the radiant flash of the rays from *the right side* of the East, informing us of the night-travelers upon the highway. The perfumed breezes of the smell of the trees aroused in us a burst of ecstasy upon a burst of ecstasy. Then we sighed and desired for our country.

Ascending during the night and redescending during the day, now, it was here, during a night of the full moon, that we saw the hoopoe entering from the opening and greeting us. In its beak, a letter, issuing *from the right side of the ridge of the valley, in a corner of the blessed ground from the tree.* The hoopoe said to us: "*I draw near you from Sheba* (Saba) *with certain tidings* in the letter from your father."

Thus it read the letter. Here is what it said: "This is addressed to you by your father, Hadi, and it is *In the Name of God the Merciful, the Compassionate.* We inspired you, but you did not show any desire. We called you, but you did not migrate. We indicated to you but you did not understand."

It continued to read the letter to us: "**You**, O such a one, if **you** wish to deliver **your**self and **your** brother, do not hold **your**self back from your decision to travel. Attach yourself to our rope and that is the Dragon of the Moon of the spiritual world which dominates the shore of the eclipse. When **you** arrive at *the Valley of the Ants*, let go of the bottom of **your** robe and say: 'Glory be to God who has made me living after having made me dead. *To Him is the Rising*.' Kill

your soul. *She will be of the ones who stay behind.* Decreed for **you** is the commandment that *the last remnant of these would be that which is severed, in that which is morning. Embark in it. In the Name of God will be the course of the ship and its berthing.*"

The Middle

The letter explained all that would happen in the course of the Way. The hoopoe went before us. The sun was in position just above our heads when we arrived at the edge of the shadows. We took our place in the ship and it carried us *amidst waves like mountains.* We intended to climb *Mount Sinai* in order to visit the hermitage of our father.

Then waves came between my son and myself. *He had been of the ones who are drowned.* I knew that for my people, *what is promised to them is in the morning. Is the morning not near?* I knew that *the town that had been doing deeds of corruption*, would be turned *its high part low*, while *rained down on it rocks of baked clay, one upon another.* When we arrived at the place where the waves dashed against each other and where the waters rolled, I took my wet-nurse and I threw her into the sea.

We voyaged upon a ship, *a vessel of planks, well-caulked.* Thus we tore the ship apart from fear of a king who came after us for *there had been a king behind taking every vessel forcefully.* The *laden boat* took us to the island of *Gog and Magog* at the left side of Mount *al-Judi*.

Then there were with me the jinn who traveled in my service. I had at my disposal the source of melting copper. I said to the jinn: *Blow until* it becomes like fire. Thus I erected a barrier (*barzakh*) to separate myself from them.

It became apparent that *the promise of my Lord had been true.* I saw in the course of the way the bones of *'Ad and Thamud.* I traveled through the region *fallen down upon its trellises.*

Then I took the two heavy things with the spheres and placed them with the jinn in a bottle which I had fabricated and given a round form and upon which there were lines designed like circles. I cut the currents of the water from the middle of the vault of heaven. When the water ceased to flow to the mill, the mill broke up and the ether escaped towards the ether. I hurled the Sphere of Spheres against the firmaments so that it crushed the sun, the moon and the stars.

Then I escaped from the fourteen coffins and the ten tombs from which emanated the shadow of God so that I would be taken towards the sacred world, being drawn *gently*. After that, I *made the sun an indicator over it*. I found the way of God and then I understood that *this is My path, straight*.

Now I had taken my sister and my family during the night and enveloped them in *the punishment from God*. They stayed plunged in a part of the very dark night with fever and nightmares until they were in a state of complete prostration.

I saw a lamp in which there was oil. Light fell from it, a light which radiated to the different parts of the house. The niche of the lamp illuminated itself and the inhabitants were embraced under the effect of the sun rising upon them.

I placed the lamp in the mouth of a dragon who inhabited the tower of the water wheel, below which I found a certain Red Sea and above which there were the stars in which no one knew the amount of their radiance except their Creator, *and those firmly rooted in knowledge*.

I saw that Leo and Taurus had both disappeared. Sagittarius and Cancer had both been hidden by the rotation of the Spheres. Libra stayed in equilibrium until the Star of Yemen had risen from behind thin clouds composed of that which was woven by the spiders of the corners of the world of the elements in the world of generation and corruption. There was also with us a ram. We abandoned him in the desert where the tremblings of the earth made it perish when lightning fell upon it. Then, when all the distance had been crossed, the road was finally terminated while *the Oven boiled* in the conic form. I saw the celestial bodies. I joined myself to them and perceived their music and their melodies. I learned their recital. The sounds were resounding in my ear like the throbbing of a chain being pulled across a hard stone.

My muscles were on the point of tearing to pieces, my joints on the point of breaking from the pleasure that I reached. The thing never ceased repeating itself to me until the white clouds were dispersed and the membrane holding the fetus in the mother's womb was torn to pieces.

The End

I left the caves and the caverns until I passed the chambers directing myself towards the Source of Life. Here I perceived the Great Rock at the peak of a mountain resembling the Sublime Mountain. I questioned the fishes that were assembled at the Source of Life, contented, taking pleasure in the shadows of the sublime lofty rock.

"That high mountain," I asked, "what is it and what is that Great Rock?"

Then *one of the fishes took its way into the sea, burrowing*. It said to me: This is what **you** desired so ardently. That mountain is Mount Sinai and the rock is the hermitage of **your** father.

"But these fish," I asked, "who are they?"

He said "They are the similarities to **your**self. You are the sons of the same father. The same thing happened to them as happened to **you**. So, they are **your** brothers."

When I heard and became certain, I embraced them. I rejoiced in seeing them as they rejoiced in seeing me. Then I ascended to the mountain. There I saw our father in the manner of a great Shaykh. The skies and the earth were almost bursting under the theophany of his light.

I stayed stupefied, astonished. I advanced towards him then he greeted me. I prostrated myself before him and I almost became annihilated in his radiant light. I cried for a time when I complained to him about the prison of Qayra-wan.

He said to me: "How well **you** have been saved, but it is absolutely necessary that **you** return to the western prison. **You** have not completely cast off the shackles."

When I heard his words, my reason took wing. I sighed while I called out like someone who is on the point of perishing and I begged him.

He said to me: "The return is absolutely necessary at this time. But I will give you two pieces of good news. The first, once **you** return to the prison it will be possible for **you** to return again to us and to mount easily towards our paradise, whenever **you** wish it. The second, it is that in the end **you** will be totally delivered to us—abandoning completely and forever the country of the West."

I became joyful upon hearing his words.

He said to me again: "Know that that mountain is Mount Sinai and above that mountain there is another mountain, *Sinin*, the home of my father and **your** ancestors. I am not in relation to him other than like **you** in relation to me. We also have other ancestors, until they reach to a King who is the Supreme Ancestor, who has neither ancestor nor father. We all are His servants. We receive and acquire our light from Him. He possesses the most sublime beauty, the highest majesty, the most captivating light. He is above the above. He is the Light of the Light and above the Light, from all eternity and for all eternity. He is the one who manifests His sacred self to all things. *The Countenance of Your Lord will remain forever* (Q55:26-27).

Epilog

I was as this state in the story when my state changed. I fell from the highest space into the abyss of the fire among the people who were not believers, as a prisoner in the country of the West, but pleasures remained with me that I am incapable of describing. I sobbed. I implored. I regreted separation. That transitory joy was one of the dreams which rapidly wears away.

   May God save us from the prison of nature and the shackles of matter. *Say: Praise belongs to God. He shall show you His signs and you will recognize them.* **Your** *Lord is not heedless of the things you do. Say: Praise belongs to God, nay, but most of them have no knowledge.*

   Blessings upon His Prophet, his family, all.

   Here ends the "Recital of the Occidental Exile."

Part Two: Translation and Commentary
"The Recital of the Occidental Exile"
In the Name of God, the Merciful, the Compassionate

Prolog

> This prolog to the "Recital of the Occidental (West) Exile" requires no commentary. Suhrawardi, while affirming his admiration, could find his point of departure, could in his turn and for his own part give an account of the journey into the Orient (East).
>
> For anyone who wishes to arrive at a concrete representation of the positive relationship between Avicenna and Suhrawardi, perhaps no better exercise in meditation could be advised than that he read the "Recital of Hayy ibn Yaqzan" and the "Recital of the Occidental Exile" in succession. H. Corbin, AVR, p. 36-37.

Thanks be to God who is the Creator of the world and blessings upon the servants whom He chose, especially upon our Sayyid, Muhammad, peace and the mercy of God be upon him, the Chosen one, his family and friends, all.

When I was reading the "Recital of Hayy ibn Yaqzan," in spite of the admirable spiritual thoughts and the profound suggestions which it contained, I found it void of lights which indicate *the Greater Catastrophe* (Q79:34).

> *When the Greater Catastrophe would draw near, on that Day the human being will recollect for what he endeavored. Hellfire will be advanced for whoever sees. As for whoever was defiant and held this present life in greater favor, then, truly, hellfire will be the place of shelter!* (Q79:34-39).
>
> When the Great Catastrophe, that is, when the theophany of the light of the essential Oneness which engulfs all things and then effaces all things and hides them, comes. TQK, Vol. 2, p 765.

In other words, the great 'stage', which is stored in the Divine Books, concealed in the symbols of the sages and hidden in the "Recital of Salman and Absal" which was composed by the same author who wrote "Hayy ibn Yaqzan." It is this secret on which are based the spiritual stations of the Sufis and of those who possess mystical intuition.

> The first part of the recital could be entitled "the fall into captivity and evasion." It is the beginning of the story of the Arif (gnostic) in that world. That episode "between two eternities" begins by the exile from the world of light, which is the East (Orient), and the captivity in the world of material physics which is the West (Occident). H. Corbin, EII, Vol. 2, p 271.

In the "Recital of Hayy ibn Yaqzan" as well, there are no indications of this except at the end of the book where it says: Sometimes certain 'unveilers' among men emigrate towards Him, etc. Thus, it was for this reason that I decided to mention a small part of that in a story that I called the "Recital of the Occidental Exile," dedicated to some of my noble friends. For my intention, I trust in God.

The Beginning
I traveled with my brother, 'Asim,

> For Suhrawardi, Asim is the faculty of contemplation which is that aspect of the soul which has no physical relationship to the body. Thus: "I traveled with my brother," means I was sheltered from the dangerous places and errors of the body. PC, OPM, p 276.

from Transoxiana

> Transoxiana, in other words, from the Transcendent world, the world of matter. The world of matter in relationship to the Transcendent world is obscure darkness. PC, OPM, p 276.

to the countries of the Occident (West)

> *The Occident (West)* ... This region is situated to the left of

the cosmos. We know that it comprises everything that exists and all beings that are connected with any kind of matter. It is perceived under a threefold aspect: (1) *the farthest Occident* of non-being, not of pure nothingness, but of pure possibility to become, perceived as the Hot Sea shrouded in Darkness. (2) *the terrestrial Occident*, where Forms that have emigrated and had been exiled into Matter ruthlessly contend against one another; (3) *the celestial Occident*, which comprises the entire system of the spheres, and whose matter is entirely different in condition from the matter of the terrestrial Occident: subtle, diaphanous, incorruptible, glorious in comparison with ours. H. Corbin, AVR, p 162.

so that we could hunt a group of birds along the shore of the Green Sea.

> By this Green Sea, the sensible world is meant. In other words: "We were looking to acquire knowledge of the senses (the birds) to discover our own perfection." From there we wished to ascend to the Angelic Intelligence and from the intellect of habit (*aql-i malakat*) and from there to the acquired intellect (*intellectus adeptus*). H. Corbin, PC, OPM p 276.

We suddenly fell into *this town whose people are ones who are unjust*, (Q4:75):

> *Why should you not fight in the way of God and for the ones taken advantage of due to weakness among the men and the women and the children, those who say: Our Lord! Bring us out from this town whose people are the ones who are unjust ...* (Q4:75).
> By a "town," this world is meant. By "the ones who are unjust," he means the people of this world. This world is a world of opposition, a coincidence of opposites. Opposition cannot exist without war and war cannot exist without injustice. PC, OPM, p. 277.

the city of Qayrawan.

> As to Qayrawan, a city in Tunisia (Kairoun), it is probably introduce because of the etymology of its name (caravan). The life of the soul in the material world is nothing but a long pil-

grimage. H. Corbin, *Journal Asiatique*, Juillet-Septembre, 1935.

The inhabitants of the city became aware of our arrival. They realized we were the sons of Shaykh Hadi ibn al-Khayr, the Yemenite.

> By "Hadi" (guide) he means the first emanation. "Khayr" (goodness) refers to the Universal Intellect. These are the means for guidance and goodness. By the chains and prison, the body is meant and by the well, this world of darkness. PC, OPM, pp 277-8.
>
> They are surrounded and enchained by the inhabitants of the town once the latter understood that the reciter and his brother are the children of the world of Light, children of Shaykh Hadi ibn al-Khayr, the Yemenite. Since they are the "children," it is he, "the father" that the exiles will rejoin at the end of this story, at the mystic *Sinin* which is at the summit of the mountain of Qaf. He indicates all three associated terms for designating the Intelligence, which are: the Angel of humanity, the Transcendent Spirit and the agent of Intelligence of the Avicennian philosophy, 10th in the angelic hierarchy. H. Corbin, EII, Vol. 2, pp 272-3.

They surrounded us and bound us in chains and shackles of iron and imprisoned us in a well whose depth was fathomless. There was directly above that well, unoccupied until peopled by our presence, a high castle.

> In other words, there were no souls which are created from material objects and bodies before we appeared. A high castle refers to the celestial spheres. PC, OPM, p 278.

fortified by a number of towers. Thus they told us: You are not forbidden to go up to the castle alone at night,

> By this is meant, at night. Through sleep one can reach the Transcendent world and see the forms of intelligibles because the senses are displaced at the time of sleeping. The senses should not prevail. In this way, you are acceptable. By day, during the time of wakefulness, because of the predominance of the senses, it is impossible that you will have the patience to

witness the intelligibles. In other words, one reaches the world of the intelligibles through death and sleep is a second death. The Quran indicates this: *God calls the souls to Himself at the time of their death and those that die not during their slumbering. He holds back those for whom He decreed death and sends the others back for a term, that which is determined. Truly, in that are signs for a folk who reflect.* (Q39:42). H. Corbin, EII, Vol. 2, p 274-5.

The captives are thrown into a deep well which culminates in the heights of a fortified castle with numerous towers. Know the castle formed the celestial Spheres and is dominated by the Fixed Stars which carry the constellations of the zodiac (the *abraj*, plural of *burj*, castle, high tower). It is permitted for the captives to climb to that castle, to endeavor the spiritual ascension of the Spheres, but only during the night. The day could appear as night and the night could appear as day, according to whether one considers the side of the "orient" or the side of the "occident." The hidden sense is that of the night of esotericism which is at the same time the day of the spiritual senses in their reality; the exoteric sense is that of the day of the exterior letter of the religious law and at the same time the darkness which surrounds the bodies, the spirits and the souls. H. Corbin, EII, Vol. 2, pp 274-5.

but when day comes, you must fall again into the bottom of the well where there were *shadows some above some others. When we put forth our hands wellnigh we could not see them* (Q24:40).

> *As for those who were ungrateful, their actions are like a mirage in a spacious plain. The thirsty one assumes it to be water until he drew near it. He finds it to be nothing. Instead, he found God with him Who paid his account in full, reckoning and God is Swift at reckoning. Or they are like the shadows in an obscure sea, overcome by a wave, above which is a wave, above which are clouds, shadows, some above some others. When he brought out his hand he almost sees it not. Whomever God assigns no light for him, there is no light for him* (Q24:39-40).

The *ungrateful* are as shadows in the depths of the fathomless sea of matter.... *The shadows* that are immerse absorb all things which come to them from the psychic faculties of the soul. They are covered by a wave of physical nature above which is the wave of the plant soul, above which are the clouds of the animal soul and its dark forms, shadows accumulated, shadows some above some others. When veiled and imprisoned by these shadows, unless he puts forth his acquired faculty and contemplates through meditation, he cannot see it (the intellect), because of the shadows and the blindness of the spiritual eye of the owner. TQK, Vol. 2, p 142.

By these shadows, matter and the impurities of material objects are meant. PC, OPM, p 219.

During the night hours we climbed to the castle, dominating the immensity of space as we looked down through an opening. Frequently doves of the forests of Yemen came and informed us of the state of things in the sacred region. Sometimes we were also visited by lights from Yemen, the radiant flash of the rays from *the right side* (Q28:30) of the East, informing us of the night-travelers upon the highway. The perfumed breezes of the smell of the trees aroused in us a burst of ecstasy upon a burst of ecstasy. Then we sighed and desired for our country.

He has said all of these things in the manner of the Arabs. By these things: ruins, traces of a dwelling, the wind and the aroma of the flowers, he remembers the Beloved. By this is meant, at the time of sleeping, we are able to perceive spiritual things and forms of the intelligibles of the spiritual world because of the putting aside of the senses. "We sighed," means we were also of that world.

Wherever Yemen or Yeman is used, it is the same. Left and left-side refer to the inferior world. PC, OPM, p 280.

To go to the right is to go upward, toward the Orient, which is the abode of pure beings of light. H. Corbin, AVR, p 157.

Ascending during the night and redescending during the day, now, it was here, during a night of the full moon, that we saw the hoopoe entering from the opening and greeting us. In its beak, a letter, issuing *from the right side of the ridge of the valley, in a corner of the blessed ground from the tree* (Q28:30).

Moses satisfied the term, he observed at the edge of the mount, from the right side of the ridge of the valley, in a corner of the blessed ground from the tree, truly and *I am God* refers to the Quranic story of Moses (Q28:29-30).

Then, when Moses satisfied the term and journeyed with his people, he observed at the edge of the mount a fire. He said to his people: Abide! Truly, I, I observed a fire so that perhaps I will bring you some news from there or burning wood of fire so that perhaps you will warm yourselves. So when he approached it, it was proclaimed from the right side of the ridge of the valley, in a corner of the blessed ground from the tree: O Moses! Truly, I am God, the Lord of the worlds (Q 28:29-30).

So *when Moses had satisfied his term*, that is, reached the extreme of perfection *and journeyed with his people*, with all his faculties in such a way that none were left behind, he went with them toward the direction of the sacred. The angel of union appeared to him being skilled in fighting and guarding him through his struggle.

He observed at the edge of the mount, that is, the mountain of the Secret which is the perfection of the heart at that height, *the fire* of the Transcendent Spirit. That is the place from where it was revealed to whomever received revelation among the Prophets.

From the right side, that is, the station of the perfection of the heart, which is called 'Secret' tree of his own sacred soul.

O Moses: Truly I am God, is the station of spiritual monologues. It is the station of having been annihilated in the attributes when both the speaker and the listener is God. TQK, Vol. 2, p 227.

By the right side, the Transcendent world is meant. TQK, Vol. 2, p 227.

The hoopoe said to us: "*I draw near you from Sheba with certain tidings*, (Q27:22):

Mention of "the hoopoe" refers to the Quranic story of Solomon, (Q27:20-22).

(Solomon) *reviewed the birds and said: Why do I not see the hoopoe bird? Had it been among the ones who are absent? I will, certainly, punish him with a severe punishment or deal a death blow to it unless it brings me a clear authority! But it was not long in coming. Then, it said: I comprehended what you have not comprehended of it. I drew near you from Sheba with certain tidings.*

(Q27:20-22)

(Solomon) *reviewed* the state of *the birds,* the spiritual faculties. He did not see *the hoopoe,* the cogitative faculty. When the cogitative faculty obeys that of instinct it becomes the estimative faculty (*wahmiyyah*) and cognition is absent, rather destroyed. It is only cognition when it is the obeyer of the intellect. *I will, certainly, punish it with a severe punishment* through strong asceticism and prohibiting the hoopoe from obeying instinct but obeying the intellect instead or *deal a death blow to it, unless it brings me a clear authority* by becoming the obeyer of the intellect because of the purity of its substance and the light of its essence. So he must bring a clear reason for its actions.

By the hoopoe he means the faculty of inspiration. "Certain news or tidings" means news of certainty and free from doubt. PC, OPM, p 280.

We have brought from Sheba (Saba) as explained in the letter from your father.

Thus it read the letter. Here is what it said: "This is addressed to you by your father, Hadi, and it is *In the Name of God the Merciful, the Compassionate* (Q27:30).

The Quranic verse: *In the Name of God, The Merciful, The Compassionate* is from the Quranic story of Solomon (Q27:28-31).

But (the hoopoe) *was not long in coming.* This means its asceticism did not take long because of its sacredness. It did not become necessary to destroy it since it returned due to its purity-with a clear excuse. His intellectual faculties practiced its excuses and chose the best one. Then (the hoopoe) said: *I comprehended what you have not comprehended of it* from the spiritual states of the city of the body and the perceptions of particulars and their mixing with universals since consciousness by itself perceives only the universals. It does not incorporate the universals to the particulars by means of a syllogism, proof or the deduction of a conclusion. It only incorporates the universals to the particulars through reflection. TBy means of meditation, consciousness apprehends the states of the Almighty and gathers together the goodnesses of the two worlds. *I drew near you from Sheba,* means the city of the body, *with certain tidings.* This means having beheld face to face through the senses. TQK, Vol. 2, p 198.

Solomon said: *Go you with this letter of mine and cast it to them. Again, turn away from them and look on what they return. She said: O Council! Truly, a generous letter was cast down to me. Truly, it is from Solomon and, truly, it is in the Name of God, The Merciful, The Compassionate. Rise not up against me, but approach me as ones who submit to God.* (Q27:28-31)

Go you with this letter of mine means practical wisdom and the Divine Law, and *cast it to them, turn away from them and look on what they return.* Will they accept obedience and submission or will they revolt? It is from Solomon, because it came from consciousness by means of meditation upon the soul. *And it is: In the Name of God, the Merciful, the Corrpassionate*, that is, in the Name of Essence through the attribute of the emanation of preparedness. It means both that which is given to things (to an object) by means of emanation to the Intellect and, that which is received of perfection from the emanation (by the subject) depending upon the suitability of one's disposition and one's attributes (or one's preparedness). *Rise not up against me*, do not dominate and raise yourself up, *but approach me as ones who submit to God*, submissive, surrendering. TQK, Vol. 2, p 201.

We inspired you, but you did not show any desire. We called you, but you did not migrate. We indicated to you but you did not understand."

It continued to read the letter to us: "**You,** O such a one, if **you** wish to deliver **your**self and **your** brother, do not hold **your**self back from your decision to travel. Attach yourself to our rope and that is the Dragon of the Moon of the spiritual world which dominates the shore of the eclipse.

If you wish to deliver yourself and your brother, in other words yourself and the contemplative faculty which is Asim. "Attach yourself ot our rope ... to the shore of the eclipse" means deliver yourself and your brother to the world of asceticism. PC, OPM, p 282.

"Attach yourself to our rope," the message says. It is exactly the response which Hermes received from his father, when he called those to his aid in the course of the perils of his ecstatic vision. There the rope was the "ray of light," the illumination of the hierarchic world. Here then, it designates something like that, but the "cryptogram'" is one of difficult reading; it is the "Dragon of the sky of the Moon of the spiritual world, which dominates the shore of the eclipse." The "deciphering" we believe could operate as follows. First of all, that which one calls in astronomy, the head and the tail of the Dragon are the "nodes of the Moon," that is to say, the points where its orbit cuts the Sun (at the moment of the eclipse). The node showing is that from which that of the Moon begins the course to the north of the elliptic, it is the head of the Dragon, the node of the north. The node descending is that part from which that of the Moon begins its course to the south of the elliptic. It is the tail of the Dragon, the node of the south.

Nevertheless, it does not end here with astronomy. The mention of the Dragon is associated with the idea of the eclipse but all fades away, to the sky of the Moon of the of the *spiritual world."* Then the Moon of the spiritual sky is none other than the mystic himself. The return of the occidental exile, is this: the eclipse or occultation to the eyes of the inhabitants of the "city of the unjust" occurs in the same way as when the mystic occults thus to his visible self and is totally invested by the light of the spiritual Sun. All the "imagery" is here coherent; he will again make mention of the Dragon at the decisive moment of the Return. H. Corbin, EII, Vol. 2, p 275-6.

When **you** arrive at *the Valley of the Ants* (Q27:18)

The words *the Valley of the Ants* refers to the Quranic story of Solomon (27:16-18).

Solomon inherited from David and he said: O humanity! We were taught the utterance of the birds and everything was given to us. Truly, this is clearly grace. There was assembled before Solomon his armies of jinn and humankind and birds and they are marching in rank until when they approached the Valley of the Ants. One ant said: O ants! Enter your dwellings so that Solomon and his armies not crush you while they are not aware. (Q27:16-18)

Ants refer to things of greed which are constantly busy gathering wealth, *O ants! Enter your dwellings so that Solomon and his armies not crush you while they are not aware!* This means hide in your residence and your quarters and return to your principles. Do this so that consciousness (Solomon) and the spiritual faculties (his hosts) will not, crush you by means of annihilation.

This is the journey of wisdom through the acquiring of virtuous habits and the adjusting of one's disposition and morals. Otherwise (that is, if one does not hide in one's residence and quarters and return to one's principles) neither Archetype nor Essence nor effect will remain for the ants, whether they be large or small, from the annihilation of the theophanies of the Attributes. TQK, Vol. 2, p 197.

let go of the bottom of **your** robe and say: 'Glory be to God who has made me living after having made me dead. *To Him is the Rising* (Q67:15).

> *It is He who made the earth submissive to you, so walk in its tracts and eat of His provision. To Him is the Rising* (Q67:15).
>
> *It is He who made* the earth of the soul *submissive to you.* Therefore, *walk* in the footsteps of your innate human nature (*fitrat Allah*) in its highest attributes, dearest corners and directions. Conquer it. Subjugate it. *Eat of His provision* which is received from His direction. This science (of Divine Nourishment) comes from the senses (as God the Most High indicated: *they would, certainly, have eaten in abundance from above them and from beneath their feet* (Q5:66)). TQK, Vol. 2, p 678.
>
> "*Valley of the Ants*" means covetness. "Let go of your robes" means desires. PC, OPM, p 282.

Kill **your** soul. *She will be of the ones who stay behind* (Q15:60 and Q29:32).

> *... but the family of Lot. Truly, we are ones who will deliver them one and all, but his woman. We ordained that she be of the ones who stay behind* (Q15:59-60).
>
> *He said: Truly, in it is Lot. They said: We are greater in knowledge of who is in it. We will, truly, deliver him and his family, but his woman. She had been among the ones who stay behind. When Our messengers drew near Lot, he was troubled because of them and he was concerned for them, distressed, and they said: Neither fear nor feel remorse. Truly, we are ones who will deliver you and your family but your woman. She had been among the ones who stay behind* (Q29:32-33).

*Then, set forth with **your** family in a part of the night and fol-low their backs and look not back any of you, but pass on to where you are commanded* (Q15:65-66).

By soul, he means the animal soul and its physical desires. PC, OPM, p 282.

The two sections which terminate the first part of the story contains the final part of the message received from the Orient and give the signs concerning the stages of the voyage. These are the "cryptograms" of the Quranic verses. *When they approached the Valley of the Ants*, seize the bottom of **your** robe," that is to say, renounce all vain discussions and recite: "*To Him is the Rising.*" The injunctions are made pressing: Kill your soul and leave your people behind to perish. That is to say, all that carries the desires of the flesh.

Here the Quranic verses are those which retell the misfor-tune which came to the wife of Lot who could never be saved because she was one of the people of Sodom who were de-stroyed by the storm raised by the sun (Q15:51-73). It is nec-essary to take one's place in the ark of Noah, which is here the mystic vessel of salvation. H. Corbin, EII, Vol. 2, pp 276-7.

Decreed for **you** is the commandment that *the last rem-nant of these would be that which is severed, in that which is morning* (Q15:66). *Embark in it. In the Name of God will be the course of the ship and its berthing* (Q11:41)."

The words: *Embark in it. In the Name of God will be the course of the ship and its berthing* refer to the Quranic story of Noah (Q11:37, 41).

Craft the boat under Our Eyes and by Our Revelation and address Me not for those who did wrong. They are, truly, ones who are drowned.... He said: Embark in it. In the Name of God will be the course of the ship and its berthing. Truly, my Lord is Forgiving, Compassionate. (Q11:37, 41)

It is possible, that according to an esoteric interpretation, the Ark symbolizes the Law brought by Noah. It was by means of this Ark that he saved himself and those with him who were among his followers. As the Prophet, peace and blessings be upon him, has said: "The people of my house, my followers, are like those of Noah's Ark. Whosoever embarks upon it, is saved and whosoever refuses is drowned."

The storm could be interpreted as the domination of the

sea of matter. The sea of matter destroys he who, among the followers of the Prophet, is not separated from it. It destroys he who has not purified his consciousness. As it has been said by Hermes, peace be upon him, in his words and his spiritual monologues, the meaning of which is: "Certainly the world is a sea full of water."

Thus if you take the ark and embark upon it, at the time of the destruction of the body, you will be saved from the sea of matter and taken back to your origin. Otherwise you will be drowned in that sea and destroyed.

(Noah) said: *Embark in it. In the Name of God will be the course of the ship and its berthing.* (Q11:41) This means that the sending of that Law (Ark) is through the Name of God, the Supreme, who is the existence of every perfect Arif (gnostic) among individuals. Invoke the Divine Name in order to penetrate into the sea of matter, in order to be able to fulfill the Divine Laws and for one's propogation into the physical world.

The evocation causes one to stand firm. It gives stability. It gives proof. The fulfillment of Divine Laws, the obeying of its rules, its very establishment and stability comes through the existence of a Prophet, or an Imam among Imams, or a saint among saintly men. TQK, Vol. 1, pp 564-5.

The Middle

The letter explained all that would happen in the course of the Way. The hoopoe went before us. The sun was in position just above our heads when we arrived at the edge of the shadows.

"The hoopoe went before us" refers to inspiration. "The sun was in position just above our heads" means our life was reaching a narrow pass, constricted. The form changed once we reached the edge of the shadow, that is, matter which is about to be disengaged from form. "When we arrived at the edge of the shadows," means the place where matter (the sun) wanted to be separated from form (the shadow). The reason for using the sun and the shadow as form and matter is His saying: *Have you not considered how your Lord stretched out the shadow? If He willed, He would make it a place of rest. Again, We made the sun an indicator over it* (Q25:47). This means that if the sun did not actively guide this shadow, matter would not have the possibility of existence. That is, it would remain a non-existent thing. PC, OPM, p 283.

We took our place in the ship and it carried us *amidst waves like mountains.* (Q11:42).

> The Quranic words: *amidst waves like mountains* refers to the Quranic story of Noah (Q11:42).
> *So it runs with them amidst waves like mountains. And Noah cried out to his son and he had been standing apart: O my son! Embark with us and be not with the ones who are ungrateful!* (Q11:42).
> *So (the ark) ran with them amidst waves,* the waves being temptations in the sea of physical nature. The waves are the instincts of physical nature which dominate over oneself, ruling through whims. The coming together of these, that is, the whims of the soul, can grow to be like mountains which veil one's sight and prevent one from journeying. Or, the waves may be interpreted as deviations from one's temperament and the domination of destructive humors. TQK, Vol. 1, p 564

We intended to climb *Mount Sinai* (Q23:20)

> The full verses are: *We caused water to descend from heaven in measure and We ceased it to dwell in the earth. We certainly are ones who have power to take away. We caused to grow for you gardens of date palm trees and grapevines where there is much sweet fruit for you and you eat of it and a tree that goes forth from Mount Sinai that bears oil and a seasoning for the ones who eat it* (Q23:18-20).
> *We caused water to descend from heaven* of the Spirit, water of the knowledge of certitude, lodged it, made it tranquil in the soul. *We certainly are ones who have power to take away* through veiling and covering. *We caused to grow for you gardens of date palm trees* of the spiritual states and divine gifts and *grapes* of good morals and good deeds, *where there is much sweet fruit* for you from the fruits of joys of the souls, hearts and the spirits, and *of them you eat,* and through them receive shelter.
> *A tree* of meditation *that goes forth from Mount Sinai* of the intellect or the mountain of the real consciousness through the intellective faculty which bears that which grows from spiritual aims which are ignited by the oil of preparedness and

clothed by the fire of the light of the Active Intellect and *seasoned* with an illuminating color. Or, *seasoned* with mystical intuition for those who have spiritual sight, the learned ones and those who seek spiritual food. TQK, Vol. 2, p 119.

in order to visit the hermitage of our father.

Then waves came between my son and myself. *He had been of the ones who are drowned* (Q11:43).

> The words: *he had been of the ones who are drowned* are from the Quranic story of Noah (Q11:43). Noah's son who drowned refers to the animal soul (*nafs al-ammarah*).
> Noah's son *said: I will take shelter for myself on a mountain. It will be what saves me from the harm of the water. Noah said: No one saves from the harm this day from the command of God but him on whom He had mercy. A wave came between them so he had been of the ones who are drowned* (Q11:43).
> Noah's son said: *I will take shelter for myself on a mountain. It will be what saves me from the harm of the water.* This means I will take refuge in the mind which is the place of reason. In other words, I will defend myself from the flood by means of reason and that which is perceived so that it will protect me from the domination by the sea of matter. Thus I will not be drowned in it.
> *Noah said: No one saves from the harm this day from the command of God but him on whom He had mercy,* except for he upon whom God has compassion through the religion of unity and the Law. *A wave came between them.* These are the waves of the soul's desires. The domination of the water of the natural sea means the wave veiled him from his father and his religion and His unity. *He was among the drowned* upon the sea of physical matter. TQK, Vol. 1, p 564.

I knew that for my people, *what is promised to them is in the morning. Is the morning not near?* (Q11:81)?

> *They said: O Lot! Truly, we are Messengers of your Lord. They will not reach out to you so set you forth with your people in a part of the night and let not any of you look back, but your woman. Truly, that which lights on them will light on her. Truly, what is promised to them is in the morning. Is the morning not near?* (Q11:81).

Is the morning not near means the time of the union of the souls—particular and universal. PC, OPM, p 284.

I knew that *the town that had been doing deeds of corruption,* (Q21:74),

> 2 *To Lot We gave him critical judgment and knowledge and We delivered him from the town which had been doing deeds of corruption. Truly, they had been a reprehensible folk, ones who disobey* (Q21:74).
> "The town" refers to the microcosm. PC, OPM, p 284.'

would be turned *its high part low* (Q11:82), while *rained down on it rocks of baked clay, one upon another* (Q11:82).

> *So when Our command drew near, We made its high part low and We rained down on it rocks of baked clay, one upon another* (Q11:82).
> "Rain" means illnesses and plagues and impurities of the base faculties like pride, stinginess and envy. PC, OPM, p 284.

When we arrived at the place where the waves dashed against each other and where the waters rolled, I took my wet-nurse and I threw her into the sea.

> "When we arrived" means when I reached a place where the temperaments were agitated, I drowned the natural spirit (foster-mother), which means, I passed from this stage. PC, OPM, p 284.

We voyaged upon a ship, *a vessel of planks, well-caulked* (Q54:13).

> *So We opened the doors of heaven with torrential water. We caused the earth to gush forth with springs so the waters were to meet one another from a command that was measured. We carried him on a vessel of planks, well-caulked* (Q54:11-13).
> "Caulked ship" means we were still with our bodies. PC, OPM, 285.

Thus we tore the ship apart from fear of a king who came after us for *there had been a king behind taking every vessel forcefully* (Q18:79).

> The words: *for behind them there was a king who was seizing every ship by brutal force* comes from the Quranic story of Moses and Khidr (Q18:79)
>
> Khidr says: I desired to damage the boat through asceticism so that the king of the corrupting soul would not seize it through force. He was the king who was behind them or in front of them, who was seizing every ship by brutal force through the predominating upon it and the using it according to its own whims and purposes.
>
> By the "king" means the angel of death. PC, OPM, p 285.
> *We rescued him and whoever was with him in the laden boat.*

The *laden boat* (Q26:119)

> Again, We drowned after that the ones who remained.
> (Q26:119-120)

took us to the island of *Gog and Magog* (Q18:94):

> *They said* with the tongue of the moment, *Gog.* That is, the natural instincts and whims of fantasy, *and Magog* the temptations and the inclinations of imagination *ones who make corruption in and on the earth* in the land of the body through the encouragement of vices and lusts contradicting the divine order, instigating activities necessitating disruption in the order; the destruction of good laws and wise rules. They bring disaster, discord, heresys which contradict justice and equity by the implying of corrupt sowing and begetting. *Will we assign to you payment* by helping you through our perfections and the forms of our perceptions against you *if you have made an embankment between us and between them* so that Gog and Magog will not transgress an obstruction that they can not surmount. That is the extent of the Law which, through practical wisdom, veils consciousness from Gog and Magog. TQK, Vol. 1, p 773-4.
>
> "Gog and Magog" means, in this spiritual state, impure thoughts and affection for this world passed through my imagination. PC, OPM, p 284.

at the left side of Mount *al-Judi* (Q11:44).

> *Mount Al-Judi* comes from the Quranic story of Noah (Q11:44).
> *It was on the same level as Al-Judi*, that is, the Law stands upon the mountain of the existence of Noah. It came to settle there.
> By the "state" he is referring to the corrupting thoughts and love of the world of his imagination.

Then there were with me the jinn:

> Jinn, in other words, the faculty of imagination. PC, OPM, pp 285-6.

who traveled in my service. I had at my disposal the source of melting copper.

> The source of melting copper means wisdom. PC, OPM, p 286.

I said to the jinn: *Blow until* (18:96) it becomes like fire. Thus I erected a barrier (*barzakh*) to separate myself from them.
It became apparent that *the promise of my Lord had been true* (Q18:98).

> He said: This barrier is the Law. *This is a mercy from my Lord.* to his servants. It causes their safety and their subsistence. So *when the promise of my Lord drew near* at the lesser judgment. *He will made it powder*, futile and demolished because of the impossibiliy of working with that barrier at the time of death and the destruction of bodily organs. *The promise of my Lord had been true.* TQK, Vol. 1, p 777.

I saw in the course of the way the bones of *'Ad and Thamud* (Q22:42).

> *That was Ad. They negated the signs of their Lord and rebelled against His Messengers. They followed the command of every*

haughty and stubborn one (Q11:59).

We sent to Thamud their brother Salih. He said: O my folk! Worship God. You have no god other than He. He caused you to grow from the earth and settled you on it. So ask for His forgiveness. Again, repent to Him. Truly, my Lord is Near, One Who Answers (Q11:61).

... as if they dwelt not in them. No doubt, truly, Thamud were ungrateful to their Lord. Away with Thamud (Q11:68).

By mentioning the bones of Ad and Thamud, he shows contempt for this world. PC, OPM p 286.

I traveled through the region *fallen down upon its trellises* (Q6:141).

> *It is He Who caused gardens to grow, trellised and without being trellised and the date palm trees and a variety of harvest crops and the olives and the pomegranates resembling and not resembling one another. Eat of its fruit when it bore fruit and give its due on the day of its reaping and exceed not all bounds. Truly, He loves not the ones who are excessive.* (Q6:141).

Then I took the two heavy things with the spheres and placed them with the jinn in a bottle which I had fabricated and given a round form and upon which there were lines designed like circles. I cut the currents of the water from the middle of the vault of heaven.

> "Two heavy things" refers to the soul which commands and the soul which blames, with their causes and reproaches. Perhaps you could translate these as understanding and imagination.
>
> "Which I had fabricated" means the brain which is the source of the energy of the psychic faculties of the soul. That is, it grows from me. "There were lines" means veins and hollows and they are like circles. "Currents of water" means the power of motion which is in the brain by means of the veins, membranes, skin and muscles. "Heaven" means the head. PC, OPM, p 286.

When the water ceased to flow to the mill, the mill broke up and the ether escaped towards the ether.

By this he means: "I overcame the psychic faculties of the soul as well." PC, OPM, p 287.

I hurled the Sphere of Spheres against the firmaments so that it crushed the sun, the moon and the stars.

This means: "I hurled the soul which commands (*nafs al-ammarah*) so that the physical spirit and the psychic faculties of the soul and the other faculties became one color. Only his special faculties such as knowledge and contemplation remained.

Then I escaped from the fourteen coffins and the ten tombs from which emanated the shadow of God.

The fourteen coffins refer to the fourteen faculties wich could be various ones such as: attraction, retention, digestion, repulsion, feeding, reproduction, retaining, growth, anger and lust in addition to the four humors (hot, cold, wet and dry). The ten tombs are the ten senses, five of which are external, five internal.PC, OPM, p 287-8.

so that I would be taken towards the sacred world, being drawn *gently* (Q20:44). After that, I *made the sun an indicator over it* (Q25:45).

Have **you** not considered how **your** Lord stretched out the shadow? If He willed, He would make it a place of rest. Again, We made the sun an indicator over it. Again, We seized it to Us an easy seizing (Q25:45-6).

Have **you** not considered **your** Lord, how He has stretched out the shadow through relative existence? Know that the quiddity of things and the reality of essences are the shadow of the Absolute and the Attributes of the knowing of the Absolute Being. Thus to stretch them out is to make them appear through His Name, Light. Light is the outward, external existence through which all things are manifested and made to appear. Non-existence overflows into the space of existence, that is, relative existence. *If He willed, He would make it a place of rest*, that is, permanently in non-existence. That is the treasury of His Being, the Mother of Books and the immutable

Guarded Tablet. The inner and real existence of everything is permanently in them. We do not mean by non-existence, absolute nothingness. Certainly, non-existence can never be actual existence. However, that which does not exist in the hidden, in the treasury of the knowledge of the Absolute and in the invisible world, can not possibly exist in the manifest world.

The bringing into existence and the taking into non-existence are nothing other than making what is immutable in the invisible, manifest and concealing that which is permanent in the hidden. *He is The First and The Last, The One Who is Outward and The One Who is Inward. And He is Knowing of everything* (57:3).

Again, We made the sun of the Intellect to the shadow, *an indicator* which leads us to knowing that the shadow's essential reality is other than its external existence. Otherwise, there is no difference between them in the external world in which nothing but existence is found. If it were not for the shadow's existence, there would not be any concrete thing in existence. Nothing but the Intellect guides us to it being something other than existence.

Thereafter *We seized it* (draw the shadow) to *Us* through annihilation drawing it with *an easy seizing* because all of the existents which are destroyed are destroyed gently by comparison to that which precedes. All things seized (withdrawn) appear almost immediately in another manifestation.

The words, to seize or to withdraw, are proof of the fact that making it disappear is not complete annihilation. Rather, the withdrawing prevents the shadow from spreading. It is withdrawn into His seizure which is the Intellect. The Intellect is the guardian of the shadow's form and its reality, eternally before and after. TQK, Vol. 2, p 160.

I found the way of God and then I understood that *this is My path, straight* (Q6:153).

> *This is My straight path, so follow it. Follow not the ways that will split you up from His way. He charged you this with it, so that perhaps you will be God-conscious* (Q6:153).
> This means the way of morality and positive traits (virtues), because the source of positive traits is unity. Do **you** not see that positive traits are the means, the intermediaries between the two extremes of excess? It is not possible in truth to actually tread the path of virtue except for those who persevere

in the religion of God. It is open only to those who are aided by God through Divine Grace to traverse the divine Path so that they reach the stage of annihilation of the attributes, that is their essence. Then one is characterized by the state of subsistence after having been annihilated in the divine attributes until one stands through God. Then he has persevered in God and through God. At this time the path is the path of the Absolute and one's journey is the journey of God.

My straight path means My way takes only he who stands by me, straightly, full of purpose, not slack towards the right and left. *Follow not the ways that will split you up from His way,* diverse paths from different idealogies and various religions for they are conventions laid down for people who are veiled by customs and desires, laid down for them so that their darkness, resistance and perplexity will not be increased. TQK, Vol. 1, p 412.

Now I had taken my sister and my family during the night and enveloped them in *the punishment from God* (Q12:107).

> *Were they safe from the approach to them of the overwhelming event of the punishment from God or the approach on them of the Hour suddenly while they are not aware?* (Q12:107).
>
> *The overwhelming event of the punishment from God* is the enveloping with a veil which hides one's being prepared to accept perfection through a fixed and dark image. TQK, Vol. 1 p 624.
>
> This means the matter of material objects of this world which remain in the world of darkness and which are capable of setting free images which Suhrawardi related to fever and nightmares. This is the interval of time when the images are not yet free. In other words, we passed beyond the matter of this world as well. PC, OPM, p 288.

They stayed plunged in a part of the very dark night with fever and nightmares until they were in a state of complete prostration.

I saw a lamp in which there was oil. Light fell from it, a light which radiated to the different parts of the house. The niche of the lamp illuminated itself and the inhabitants were embraced under the effect of the sun rising upon them.

> "The lamp" means the Active Intellect which is the master of this world. It is active in the sense that many works are born from it in contrast to the intelligibles of the spheres which give birth to only one act. That oil which is born from it refers to the power of subsistence of physical bodies. The body is known as the kingdom. PC, OPM, p 289.

I placed the lamp in the mouth of a dragon who inhabited the tower of the water wheel, below which I found a certain Red Sea and above which there were the stars in which no one knew the amount of their radiance except their Creator, *and those firmly rooted in knowledge* (Q3:7).

> *It is He who caused the Book to descend to you. In it are signs, ones that are definitive. They are the essence of the Book and others, ones that are unspecific. Then, those whose hearts are swerving, they follow what was unspecific in it, looking for dissent and looking for an interpretation, but none knows its interpretation but God. The ones who are firmly rooted in knowledge say: We believed in it as all is from our Lord. None recollects, but those imbued with intuition* (Q3:7)
>
> *In it are signs, ones that are definitive*, more sublime, so that probability and error do not find their way to them. They that only have one meaning. *They are the essence of the Book.* That is, the principal of the Book *and others, ones that are unspecific* which have two or more meanings. Truth and falsehood can be confused in them. This is so because the Transcendent Absolute has one Face. It is the Face of the Absolute which abides after the annihilation of the creature. It does not accept multiplicity and diversity. But He has multiple, relative faces, in accordance with the many mirrors of manifestation. This relative face or aspect is that which appears in every manifestation according to the preparedness (inner, essential capacity) of every theophany. From that single manifestation, truth is mingled with falsehood. Each manifestation is related to the relative face which suits it. Hence follows trial and testing.
>
> But the veritable Arifs (gnostics) are those who are able to recognize the abiding Face in every form in which it is manifested. They know the Face of the Absolute from the faces

which are carried in the ambiguous verses. So they take them
back to the clear verses. In this they follow the examples of the
poet who says: "There is no Face but One except that when
you count the mirrors of manifestation they increase." But the
veiled ones, as for *those whose consciousness is swerving* from the
Absolute, *they follow what was unspecific in it* because of their
being veiled from unity by multiplicity. The veritable Arifs
(gnostics) instead, follow the clear verses and make the ambiguous ones follow the lead of the clear ones. Thus they choose,
among the possible faces, that which corresponds to religion
and faith.

 Looking for dissent means seeking to go astray and mis-
leading those who are upon the way, *looking for an interpretation* corresponding to their spiritual state and their methods.
As the saying goes: When the sword becomes crooked, the
sheath also changes shape. As they do not know the abiding
Face among the faces, it follows that they do not know the
true meaning from the meanings. That is why their veils increase and become denser until because of that they become
deserving of chastisement.

 *None knows its interpretation but God and the ones who are
firmly rooted in knowledge.* The knowers who know through the
knowledge of God, means, certainly, God knows totally and in
detail. They say: "We believe in it," and by this they verify the
knowledge of God about it. Thus they know through the light
of faith. *All is from our Lord* because to them all has one and
the same meaning which does not vary. Yet *none recollects* this
single, discriminative knowledge in the manifold ambiguous
verses *but those imbued with intuition* who have been cleansed
by the light of guidance and who have been separated from
the shell of desires and habits. TQK, Vol. 1, p 167.

 This means the Active Intellect which is the master of this
world: "I left as well, with the elements of this world." The reason for this is that he has said "inhabited" and the elements of
this world, even though they rotate, they do not look like circles.

 By the water tower, the firmaments is meant, in other
words, the water wheel is turned and the firmaments turn.
When he says: "Below which I found a certain Red Sea," he
means that it is through water that the firmaments descend.
Above it the stars is in itself apparent. In other words, from this
world and from the Active Intellect I also passed and reached
the celestial Sphere and its bodies. PC, OPM, pp 289-90.

I saw that Leo and Taurus had both disappeared. Sagittarius and Cancer had both been hidden by the rotation of the Spheres. Libra stayed in equilibrium until the Star of Yemen had risen from behind thin clouds composed of that which was woven by the spiders of the corners of the world of the elements in the world of generation and corruption.

> "Even though the name of Leo and Taurus remained separate," means that we reached the world of immaterial bodies, the word of singularities, having one nature is not a war as between the bull and lion. "Sagittarius and Cancer had both been hidden ..." means no crookedness remained since these two indicate crookedness. By the "Star of Yemen" the Universal Soul is meant. Then he says: "From behind thin clouds," which means outside of form. That is the Intellect and the Soul. Those clouds are the webs which the spiders of the corners of the world of elements weave. PC, OPM, p 290.

There was also with us a ram. We abandoned him in the desert where the tremblings of the earth made it perish when lightning fell upon it. Then, when all the distance had been crossed, the road was finally terminated while *the Oven boiled* (Q11:40 and Q23:27) in the conic form.

> *Until, when Our command came, and the Oven boiled ...* (Q11:43) Boiled in the oven of the body (and thus cleansed) from the domination of a corrupt temperament and the excess of humidity upon the natural temperature when the watery nature of "matter" becomes stronger than the fire of the animal spirit. Or, the perishing spiritually when the oven boils by the predominance of water upon the natural desires of the heart and the drowning of (those desires) in the physical sea of "matter." TQK, Vol. 1, p 562.

I saw the celestial bodies. I joined myself to them and perceived their music and their melodies. I learned their recital. The sounds were resounding in my ear like the throbbing of a chain being pulled across a hard stone.

My muscles were on the point of tearing to pieces, my joints on the point of breaking from the pleasure that I reached. The thing never ceased repeating itself to me until the white clouds were dispersed and the membrane holding the fetus in the mother's womb was torn to pieces.

The preceding has been a rapid triumph of the liturgical recital of the Quran, realizing in a few sections, the state of the perfect story, defined here precisely as a trinity realized in the actual recital, the trinity of the reciter, of the gesture sited and of the heros whose story is recited. It is not the historic and archeological sense of the Quran which is recited by the reciter of the Occidental Exile. Suhrawardi puts the work in its proper perspective: Recite the Quran as if it were revealed for **your** own case. The Shaykh of Ishraq suffices, by himself alone, to show that there has never been an incompatibility between the spatial schematization of the Platonic Above and the temporal schematization of the anthropological Quran or Bible of the Above. It is, in effect, precisely that space which is the work of that field of that story, he permits it to have always an instant to go beyond itself and to repeat itself, brief by not being a chronicler but a liturgy, a liturgy realizing the reversibility of time in the space brought into being by time itself. By the liturgical recital of the Quranic verses, the reciter comes to revive the drama of the prophets; in his voyage to the mystic Sinai he follows from prophet to prophet of his being, rolled up from sky to sky of his being, until the *astrum in homine*. H. Corbin, EII, Vol. 2, pp 278-9.

The End

I left the caves and the caverns until I passed the chambers directing myself towards the Source of Life. Here I perceived the Great Rock at the peak of a mountain resembling the Sublime Mountain.

The Sublime Mountain refers to *Sinin* through his human imagination. The imagination is a concentrated extract of physical and spiritual energies. The pilgrim at the foot of Sinin now finds himself is a mystic Sinin, that which culminates at the summit of Mount Qaf and at that summit of that Sinai there is the Great Rock which is the oratory of the Angel, which is that key of the vault of the world of the Spheres, "the celestial door," and at the same time, the passage towards the Above, towards Na-koja-abad (the country of Nowhere, the 8th clime which is represented as being on the convex surface of the sphere of Spheres; that is not only, understand well, a "means of speech"). It is why the pilgrim makes the ascension. There also is the limit between the visible and the suprasensible world, and it is to that limit which produces itself in the encounter between the terrestial I and his celestial I, the "Angel" that he goes. One can only succeed to it after having bathed in the Source of Life. H. Corbin, EII, Vol. 2, p 282.

I questioned the fishes that were assembled at the Source of Life, contented, taking pleasure in the shadows of the sublime lofty rock.

"That high mountain," I asked, "what is it and what is that Great Rock?"

Then *one of the fishes took its way into the sea, burrowing* (Q18:61).

> The words: *it took to itself a way through the sea, burrowing* is from the Quranic story of Moses and Khidr (Q18:60-82)
>
> Moses was asleep when the fish took its way into the sea as has been said, whereas the page, the soul was awake. The Satan of fantasy which embellished the tree for Adam made Moses forget to remind the soul of the fish because Moses was in a state of negligence and forgetfulness. The way in which they were wandering refers to the large hole mentioned above. Said (Moses), *This* (the fish's taking its way to freedom) *is what we have been seeking*, looking for because it was at the meeting of the two seas where Moses had been promised a meeting with the being who is more knowing than he.

It said to me: This is what **you** desired so ardently. That mountain is Mount Sinai and the rock is the hermitage of **your** father.

"But these fish," I asked, "who are they?"

He said "They are the similarities to **your**self. You are the sons of the same father. The same thing happened to them as happened to **you**. So, they are **your** brothers."

When I heard and became certain, I embraced them. I rejoiced in seeing them as they rejoiced in seeing me. Then I ascended to the mountain. There I saw our father in the manner of a great Shaykh. The skies and the earth were almost bursting under the theophany of his light.

I stayed stupefied, astonished. I advanced towards him then he greeted me. I prostrated myself before him and I almost became annihilated in his radiant light. I cried for a time when I complained to him about the prison of Qayrawan.

He said to me: "How well **you** have been saved, but it is absolutely necessary that **you** return to the western prison, **you** have not completely cast off the shackles."

When I heard his words, my reason took wing. I sighed while I called out like someone who is on the point of perishing and I begged him.

He said to me: "The return is absolutely necessary at this time. But I will give you two pieces of good news. The first, once **you** return to the prison it will be possible for **you** to return again to us and to mount easily towards our paradise, whenever **you** wish it. The second, it is that in the end **you** will be totally delivered to us—abandoning completely and forever the country of the West."

I became joyful upon hearing his words.

He said to me again: "Know that that mountain is Mount Sinai and above that mountain there is another mountain, *Sinin* (Q95:2), the home of my father and **your** ancestors. I am not in relation to him other than like **you** in relation to me.

> By the fig and the olive and by Mount Sinin and by this trustworthy land ... (Q95:1-3)

Mount Sinin means the brain which is the source of the senses and the imagination which rises from the earth of the body like a mountain. TQK, Vol. 2, P 825.

"Ancestors" means the Universal Intellect and emanation. And this father is not of the type to have a consort as fools say, because they (father and ancestors) do not save the reproductive faculty since they are not capable of composition or solution "I am not in relation to him other than like you in relation to me," means we are both images and the difference is just that, that you are a piece and I am a collector of you. PC, OPM, p 295.

We also have other ancestors, until they reach to a King who is the Supreme Ancestor, who has neither ancestor nor father. We all are His servants. We receive and acquire our light from Him. He possesses the most sublime beauty, the highest majesty, the most captivating light. He is above the above. He is the Light of the Light and above the Light, from all eternity and for all eternity. He is the one who manifests His sacred self to all things. *The Countenance of Your Lord will remain forever* (Q55:26-27).

> *All who are in or on it are ones who are being annihilated, yet the Countenance of thy Lord will remain forever, Possessor of The Majesty and The Splendor* (Q55:26-7).
>
> *All who are in or on it are ones who are being annihilated.* All who are upon the traveling vessels are united with the Absolute through annihilation in Him. Or, all things which are in the earth of the body, from the permanent possibilities, like the spirit, the intellect, the heart and the soul and its stages, stations and degrees, perish at the time of uniting with the purpose.
>
> *Yet the Countenance of thy Lord will remain forever,,* subsisting after annihilation of the creature, that is, His Essence, with all of the attributes. Majestic means great, sublime through the veiling by the light and darkness of the veils and the manifestation of the essence through the attributes of kindness and compassion. TQK, Vol. 2, p 574.
>
> "Supreme Ancestor" means His greatness and this greatness is greater and it is not a part (of something else). PC, OPM, p 296.

Epilog

I was as this state in the story when my state changed. I fell from the highest space into the abyss of the fire among the people who were not believers, as a prisoner in the country of the West, but pleasures remained with me that I am incapable of describing. I sobbed. I implored. I regreted separation. That transitory joy was one of the dreams which rapidly wears away.

May God save us from the prison of nature and the shackles of matter. *Say: Praise belongs to God. He shall show you His signs and you will recognize them.* **Your** *Lord is not heedless of the things you do* (Q27:95 and Q 31:25). *Say: Praise belongs to God, nay, but most of them have no knowledge.*

Blessings upon His Prophet, his family, all.

Here ends the "Recital of the Occidental Exile."

Recapitulation[1]

In his treatise *al-Qissat al-Ghurbat al-Gharbiyyah*, the "Recital of the Occidental Exile," in which Suhrawardi seeks to reveal the secrets of the trilogy of ibn Sina, the universe becomes a crypt through which the seeker after truth must journey, beginning with this world of matter and darkness into which he has fallen and ending in the Orient of lights, the original home of the spirit, which symbolizes illumination and spiritual realization. The journey begins at the city of Qairawan in present-day Tunis, located west of the main part of the Islamic world. The disciple and his brother are imprisoned in the city at the bottom of a well which means the depth of matter. They are the sons of Shaikh Hadi ibn al-Khair al-Yamani, i.e., from the Yaman, which in Arabic means also the right hand and, therefore, symbolically the Orient, and is connected traditionally with the wisdom of the Prophet Solomon and the ancient sages as the left is connected with matter and darkness.

Above the well is a great castle with many towers, i.e., the world of the elements and the heavens or the faculties of the soul. They will be able to escape only at night and not during the day which means that man reaches the intelligible or spiritual world only in death, whether this be natural or initiatory, and in a dream which is a second death. In the well there is such darkness that one cannot see even one's own hands, i.e., matter is so opaque that rarely does light shine through it. Occasionally they receive news from the Yaman which makes them homesick, meaning that they see the intelligible world during contemplation or in dreams. And so, they set out for their original home.

One clear night an order is brought by the hoopoe from the Governor of the Yaman (the right side, the East, the Orient) telling them to begin their journey to their homeland, meaning the reception of a revelation from the intelligible world and the beginning of asceticism. The order also asks them to let go the hem of their dress, i.e., become free from attachment, when they reach the valley of ants, which is the passion of avidity. They are to kill their souls, i.e., passions or animal soul, and then sit in a ship and begin their journey in the *name* of God. Having made their preparation they set out for their pilgrimage to Mount Sinai.

A wave comes between the disciple and the son, meaning that the animal soul is sacrificed. Morning is near, that is, the union of the particular soul with the universal soul is approaching. The hero discovers that the world in which evil takes place, meaning this world, will be overturned and rain and stones, i.e., diseases and moral evils, will descend upon it.

Upon reaching a stormy sea he throws in his foster-mother and drowns her, meaning that he even sacrifices his natural soul. As he travels on still in storm, i.e., in the body, he has to cast away his ship in fear of the king above him who collects taxes, meaning death which all mortals must taste. He reaches the Mount of Gog and Magog, i.e., evil thoughts and love of this world enter his imagination. The jinn, the powers of imagination and meditation, are also before him as well as a spring of running copper which symbolizes wisdom.

The hero asks the jinn to blow upon the copper which thus becomes fiery, and from it he builds a dam before Gog and Magog. He takes the carnal soul (animal soul, *nafs ammarah*) and places it in a cave, or the brain which is the source of this soul. He then cuts the "streams from the liver of the sky," i.e., he stops the power of motion from the brain which is located in the head, the sky of the body. He throws the empyrean heaven so that it covers all the stars, the sun, and the moon, meaning all powers of the soul become of one color, and passes by fourteen coffins, the fourteen powers of *ishraqi* psychology, and ten tombs, the fire external and the five internal senses.

Having passed through these stages he discovers the path of God and realizes that it is the right path. The hero passes beyond the world of matter and reaches a light, the active intellect which is the governor of this world. He places the light in the mouth of a dragon, the world of the elements, and passes by it to reach the heavens and beyond them to the signs of the Zodiac which mark the limit of the visible cosmos. But his journey is not yet at an end; he continues even beyond them to the upper heavens. Music is heard from far away, and the initiate emerges from the cavern of limitation to the spring of life flowing from a great mountain which is Mount Sinai. In the spring he sees fish that are his brothers; they are those who have reached the end of the spiritual journey.

He begins to climb the mountain and eventually reaches his father, the archangel of humanity, who shines with a blinding light which nearly burns him. The father congratulates him for having escaped from the prison of Qairawan, but tells him that he must return because he has not yet cast away all bonds. When he returns a second time, he will be able to stay. The father tells him that above them is his father, the Universal Intellect, and beyond him their relatives going back to the Great Ancestor who is pure light. "All perishes except His essence."

*****

From this brief summary we see how *ishraqi* wisdom implies essentially a spiritual realization above and beyond discursive thought. The cosmos becomes transparent before the traveler and interiorized within his being. The degrees of realization from the state of the soul of fallen man to the center of the soul freed from all limitation corresponds "horizontally" to the journey from the Occident of matter to the Orient of lights, and "vertically" to the ascent from the earth to the limits of the visible universe and from there, through the world of formless manifestation, to the divine essence.

Endnote

1 Seyyed Hossein Nasr, "Shihab al-Din Suhrawardi Maqtul," in M. M. Sharif, *History of Muslim Philosophy*. Online. Footnotes not included.

Bibliography

Bakhtiar, Laleh, *Laleh Bakhtiar, Ph.D. Letters Volume 5*.
	Chicago: Kazi Publications, 2019.
— *Quranic Psychogy of the Self: A Textbook on Islamic Moral
	Psychology*. Chicago: Kazi Publications, 2019.
— *The Sublime Quran*. Chicago: Kazi Publications, 2007.
Corbin, Henry, *Avicenna and the Visionary Recitals*. Princeton:
	Princeton University Press, 1980.
— *En Islam Iranien, II, Sohrawardi et les Platoniciens de Perse*.
	Paris: Gallimard, 1991.
— *Oeuvres philosophiques et mystiques de Shiabbadin Yahya
	Sohrawardi*. Tehran: Franco-Iranian Institute, 1968.
Nasr, Seyyed Hossein, *History of Muslim Philosophy*. Online.
— *Three Muslim Sages*, Michigan: Caravan Press, 1969.

Other Books in the Great Books of the Islamic World Series
al-Ghazzali Jewels of the Quran
al-Ghazzali Just Balance
al-Ghazzali On Being a Muslim
al-Ghazzali On Disciplining the Self
al-Ghazzali On Enjoining Good and Forbidding Wrong
al-Ghazzali On Hope and Fear
al-Ghazzali On Knowing This World and the Hereafter
al-Ghazzali On Knowing Yourself and God
al-Ghazzali On Listening to Music
al-Ghazzali On Love, Longing and Contentment
al-Ghazzali On Marriage
al-Ghazzali On Patience and Gratitude
al-Ghazzali On Reckoning and Guarding
al-Ghazzali On Repentance
al-Ghazzali On Sufism
al-Ghazzali On the Duties of Brotherhood
al-Ghazzali On the Lawful, the Unlawful and the Doubtful
al-Ghazzali On the Treatment of Anger, Hatred and Envy
al-Ghazzali On the Treatment of Hypocrisy
al-Ghazzali On the Treatment of Ignorance Arising from
        Heedlessness, Error and Delusion
al-Ghazzali On the Treatment of Love for This World
al-Ghazzali On the Treatment of Love of Power
     and Control
al-Ghazzali On the Treatment of Miserliness and Greed
al-Ghazzali On the Treatment of Pride and Conceit
al-Ghazzali On the Treatment of the Harms of the Tongue
al-Ghazzali On the Treatment of the Lust of the Stomach
     and the Sexual Organs
al-Ghazzali On Trust and the Unity of God
al-Ghazzali On Truthfulness and Sincerity
al-Ghazzal Other Daily Acts of Worship
al-Ghazzali Recitation and Interpretation of the Quran
al-Ghazzali The Alchemy of Happiness Abridged, pbk.
al-Ghazzali The Alchemy of Happiness, 2 vols. pbk, hbk
al-Ghazzali Mysteries of the Human Soul

al-Farabi, On the Perfect State
al-Qushayri, The Risalan

al-Qushayri, Sufi Book of Spiritual Ascent

Avicenna On Aphrodisiacs and their Medical Uses
Avicenna On Cardiac Drugs
Avicenna On Childbirth
Avicenna On Cosmetics and their Medicinal Uses
Avicenna On Diagnosis Signs and Symptoms
Avicenna On Diagnosis The Pulse
Avicenna On Diseases Causes and Symptoms
Avicenna On Exercising, Massaging, Bathing, Eating,
Drinking, Sleeping, Fatigue
Avicenna On Illness
Avicenna On Managing the Elderly, Temperament
        Extremes, Environmental Changes
Avicenna On Medicine and Its Topics
Avicenna On the Four Elements
Avicenna On the Four Humours
Avicenna On the Four Temperaments
Avicenna On the Healing Properties of Minerals, Plants
        and Animals
Avicenna On the Science of the Soul
Avicenna On Treating Arthritis and the Joints
Avicenna On Treating the Organs of the Head
Avicenna On Treating Swellings and Pimples
Avicenna On Treating the Alimentary Organs and Diet
Avicenna On Treating the Excretory Organs
Avicenna On Treating the Respiratory Organs
        and the Chest
Avicenna On Treating the Visual Organs
Avicenna On Treating Wounds and Ulcers
Avicenna On the Breath
Avicenna On the Three Faculties
Avicenna On Theology
Avicenna On Therapeutics for Diseases, Disorders, Obstructions,
Swellings, Managing Pain
Avicenna, Poem on Medicine
Avicenna, Canon of Medicine Volume 1: General Medicine hbk
Avicenna, Canon of Medicine Volume 2: Natural
        Pharmaceuticals hbk
Avicenna, Canon of Medicine Volume 3: Special

Pathologies hbk
Avicenna, Canon of Medicine Volume 4: Systemic Diseases,
    Orthopedics and Cosmetics hbk
Avicenna, Canon of Medicine Volume 5: Pharmacopia hbk
Avicenna, Canon of Medicine 5 Volume Set hbk

Abul Qasim al-Iraqi, Cultivation of Gold

Divine Flashes of Husayn

Ibn Arabi On the Mysteries of Bearing Witness pbk, hbk.
Ibn Arabi On the Mysteries of Fasting pbk
Ibn Arabi On the Mysteries of the Pilgrimage pbk
Ibn Arabi On the Mysteries of the Purifying Alms pbk
Ibn Arabi On the Mysteries of Purity and Formal Prayer pbk
Ibn Arabi, Ringstones of Wisdom (*Fusus al-Hikam*)
Ibn Arabi, Unveiling the Secret of the Most Beautiful Names pbk

Ibn Miskawayh, Refinement of Character by Ibn Miskawayh

Ibn Nadim, Fihrist, al-

Kamal al-Din Husayn Kashifi, Royal Book of Spiritual Chivalry

Life After Death, Resurrection, Judgment and the Final Destiny
    of the Soul Vol. 1 pbk hbk
Life After Death, Resurrection, Judgment and the Final Destiny
    of the Soul Vol. 2 pbk hbk

Muhammad Kisai, Tales of the Prophets

Razi's Traditional Psychology

Rumi *Mathnawi* Complete in French, 3 Vols hbk
Rumi *Mathnawi* Complete in Spanish, 3 Vols hbk
Rumi *Mathnawi* Complete in German, 3 Vols hbk
Rumi *Mathnawi* Complete in Swedish, 3 Vols hbk
Rumi *Mathnawi* Complete in Italian, 3 Vols hbk